Ascending into Euphoria

Ascending into Euphoria

A COLLECTION OF POETRY

Tiffany Tinney

Order this book online at www.trafford.com
or email orders@trafford.com

Most Trafford titles are also available at major online book retailers.

Printed in the United States of America.

ISBN: 978-1-4269-6691-0 (sc)
ISBN: 978-1-4269-6693-4 (e)

Library of Congress Control Number: 2011908190

Trafford rev. 12/28/2011

 www.trafford.com

North America & international
toll-free: 1 888 232 4444 (USA & Canada)
phone: 250 383 6864 ♦ fax: 812 355 4082

Table of Contents

The Poet   ix

Section One: Poetry Expressed through Nature   1

The Love of Nature   2

Indian Paintbrush   3

Fallen Colors   4

A Loner   5

Spring Haiku   8

Spring Haiku II   9

Autumn Haiku   10

Halloween Haiku   11

The Essence of Beauty   12

Native America   13

Red Is for Apple   14

Uncivilized   15

The Morning Dew   16

A Summer's Dream   17

Section Two: Potluck Poetry   18

Nonsense   19

Nonsense II   20

Painful Breakup   21

Elwood Pines   22

Creatures   23

The Small Things in Life   24

Prince Charming   25

The Taste of Sweetness   26

Wedded Bliss   27

A Star   28

Section Three: Poems of the Heart   **29**

You   30

Real Love Doesn't Hurt   31

I Tell You, "I Love You"   32

A Loss for Words   33

The Best   35

Another Sappy Love Poem   36

My Choice   37

Thanks for Nothing   39

A Chance   40

Section Four: Poems of my Life, My Thoughts, And Me   **41**

The Life I've Never Known   42

This Incredible Woman   44

9-11-01   46

Note to Jerry Falwell   47

Troubled World   48

The Color Black   49

Loneliness Is a Disease   51

Today Is My Birthday   52

A Small Prayer   53

My Virginity   55

The Last Afternoon of My Life   57

Maybe It's Better   58

Nobody's Perfect   59

For Amber Grace Brown, a.k.a. "Pamps," because I promised you.
For my mom, Grace Ann Tinney, thanks for believing in me.

The Poet

In evening shadows
      of the skylight's radiance,
            the Poet ascends into euphoria.

Section One:

Poetry Expressed Through Nature

The Love of Nature

Sunshine and the ocean breeze,
I'm with you, and I feel these.

Blades of grass and sands of grain,
you're with me and I see no rain.

The summer ends and autumn starts,
we've just met, but you took my heart.

Trees in the wind, rocks in the stream,
I've known you forever, it seems.

A hyena's laugh, a wolf's howling cry,
I like you a lot, but I wonder why.

Smile of an angel, sweetness of a baby,
could this be the attraction? I don't know—maybe.

Hair like Black Beauty, sparkling eyes like a jewel,
honey, whatever the reason is, I really like you.

Indian Paintbrush

Indian paintbrush red
blended across the sky
of a golden setting sun

White angelic clouds
floating in the sky
of an ocean blue

Forests of emeralds
reaching out to the sky
of a silver rising moon

Fallen Colors

Fallen leaves are like friends
that slowly drift through your life.
Red leaves are for the past lovers that
still appear in your mind.
Yellow leaves are for the close friends
from childhood who always seemed to make you smile.
Orange leaves are for the old friends
that resurface in your life from time to time.
Brown leaves are for the people who you thought were friends,
that are all but dead to you now.
Green leaves in the spring will bring new
friendships that in time will change to their own
fallen colors.

A Loner

I feel so strange and weak;
there's not a light on down my street.

I feel so weird and cold
when it's dark all down my road.

Can someone show me the way
so maybe I won't have to stray?

Faintly, I think I hear a sound;
it's just a raindrop on the ground.

It's going to start pouring soon,
as I stand here under the moon.

There's no one in my touch or sight,
I'm alone in the world tonight.

While everyone else is in bed,
I sit here and wonder in my head.

What is life all about?
Can someone help me figure it out?

I hear the whistling wind—
what kind of situation am I in?

If you look up at the brightest star,
you can almost see who you truly are.

I go and lie down under a tree
and ponder what is happening to me.

All I do is sit and stare—
is there anybody out there?

The temperature is dropping down
as more rain falls to the ground.

The raindrops that are hitting my nose—
in the springtime will bloom a rose.

A flash of lightning streaks the sky
as I sit here and I sigh.

The storm is getting stronger;
I can't stay out much longer.

When I am not inside,
my dreams are where I hide.

When I'm in my thoughts I feel so free,
I can truly be who I want to be.

I'm inside now, but before I close the door,
I take one last look as raindrops pour.

Sadly, as I go to bed, my dreams I shake.
Maybe I'll dream some more before I wake.

In my own way I'm unique.
I walk to the drum of a different beat.

I don't care what people think or say,
I like myself and I'll stay this way.

You see, I'm a dream owner,
and yes, it's true, I'm a loner.

Spring Haiku

Fuchsia and white blooms
entwined on a lengthy bark,
wrapped in harmony.

Spring Haiku

Lilac and green shades
of mossy grass in the spring
by a lake of blue.

Autumn Haiku

Leaves fall to the ground,
red, yellow, orange, and brown,
without noise, or sound.

Halloween Haiku

The moon shines brightly;
the winds blow, howl, groan, and moan,
as the ghosts come out.

The Essence of Beauty

I love the earth.
She is my mother,
my soul,
my inner beauty,
my essence and my life.
Without her I could not breathe,
I couldn't smell, couldn't see.
The birds, the sea, the grass,
everything belongs to her.
My mother, my earth.

Native America

A harvest moon reminds me
of ancient America,
native America.
When natives would sit around
a fire circle
chanting and meditating.
They give thanks to the gods
for the summer crops
and pray that they will
be merciful enough
to keep them
throughout the winter.

Red Is for Apple

R
E
D

in every bite. is for apple

good   sweet

taste   and

They   round.

ripe.   You

and   can

juicy   find

sweet   them

are   on

Apples .ground the

Uncivilized

When I sip water,
I think of how pure
it must have been,
thousands of years ago.
I see rivers flowing from
unpolluted streams,
so clean,
so fresh.
Wondering what it must
have felt like to bathe
underneath a waterfall,
of something
so new and untouched.
What a beautiful sight,
those waters.
Now we use filters for clean water.
Now all of the rivers are
green and polluted.
Some things in civilization
are best uncivilized.

The Morning Dew

The dew on the morning grass,
shines in the yellow sun.
It glistens with great beauty,
which never seems overdone.

It reflects like a rainbow.
It's odd how it came to be
that something that is so small
can truly mesmerize me.

A Summer's Dream

Quiet.
Forest leaves blowing
in the breeze.
Sun shining through
the foggy mist
of the morning dew.
Animals scurrying about
on the forest floor.
Cries echo
throughout the land.
Trees lending shelter to
even the tiniest insect.
Light fades away
with the evening sun.
Everything heads for home
as the rain starts to pour
on the forest bed.

Section Two:

Potluck Poetry

Nonsense

Blinking eyes,
dancing clowns,
little babes
crying out.

Headless men,
hero's sigh,
gorgeous eagle,
watchful eye.

Lady in red,
bride in white,
a strange man
is out tonight.

Nonsense

Blond hair,
green eyes.
What a day.
What a surprise.

Why now?
Why today?
You came over
but did not stay.

Big feet,
small hands,
so perfect,
yet not a man.

Fly away,
swim fast.
Not so good—
you came in last.

Painful Breakup

Only YOU
saw the sensation
and despair
that ripped into
my desire
like really sick
ravages
and senseless
good-byes.

Elwood Pines

The waves break
incessantly
as we laugh beneath
desired love.
We have wild nights
and conversations
under the stars
in Elwood Pines.

Creatures

Salamanders and ravens wait
like black murky shadows
with primitive
seducing minds.

The Small Things in Life

The smell of restaurant food in the air when you are driving by.
The idea of being able to go out with your friends.
Growing up.
Your own apartment.
Dog and/or cat.
Busch Gardens.
New big houses.
Just driving.
Looking up at the clouds.
Being in the woods, surrounded by trees.
Walking on the dock.
Swimming.
Going to the beach.
Sun tans.
Going shopping at the mall.
Movies.
Fresh air.
Jewelry.
Fake and real tattoos.
Water.
Nature.
Beauty.
Falling asleep.
Going to your first party.
Going to your first concert.
First date.
Feeling of serenity.
New makeup.
The feeling when you're fresh out of the shower.
Washing your hair.
Loving life.

Prince Charming

You hear the words a thousand times—
they forever ring out in your mind.
You're searching for what you cannot find,
you're racing through the sands of time
to find the one who truly cares.
In your heart you know he's there.
You look all around you and wonder, "Where?"
Then you finally give up, with despair.

The Taste of Sweetness

The taste of sweetness,
it is so divine.
The feeling of our love
between your heart and mine.

Your arms around me,
holding on so tight.
I love the look in your eyes
as we make love through the night.

Wedded Bliss

Love that is so true
can be hard to find.

If you keep your love new,
it will grow in due time.

Keep your minds and souls together,
and nothing will tear you apart.

I hope that your love lasts forever,
and you keep nothing but joy in your hearts.

A Star

There once was a girl who loved to sing.
She knew it was her everything.

But the little girl was very shy.
When she sang solo, she'd cry.

One day, some songs she began to write,
and she realized the dream she had in sight.

She wanted to become a star,
and being scared wouldn't get her far.

She decided to get rid of the fright
and pushed her dream with all of her might.

Now she has come very far;
and soon she will become a star.

Section Three:

Poems Of The Heart

You

Lying here
warm and cozy in my bed,
I'm listening to you breathe in my ear
while you sleep.
It's soothing.
Any other night
I'd try to wake you
because your phone will be dead in the morning.
But tonight,
there's something special.
There's a vulnerability in your sound,
like that of a baby,
and I've never known that in you.
I'm cherishing this moment because
I know it will be a while before I will
feel this close to you again.
In my mind,
I'm wishing you were here
so I could watch you dream,
play with your hair,
kiss your cheek,
then whisper, "I love you,"
knowing that when I say that,
you will never fully realize just
how much you mean to me
and how much I really do care.
And sadly,
I know that tomorrow
you'll go back to being the same old
tough, stubborn, macho **YOU**
that I know so well.

Real Love Doesn't Hurt

I love you, but you hurt me.
The things you say make me cry.
I put up with you, and I don't know why.
I love you, but you hurt me.
I'm in pain here, can't you see?
It's not funny—it's not a game to me.
I love you, but you hurt me,
and I realize I'm a precious jewel.
So I've got news for you: we're through.
I love you, but you hurt me.
Now you say you love me, but you don't mean what you say—
if you truly loved me, you'd show me another way.
I love you, but you hurt me.
You say, "No, we can make this work."
I love you, but you hurt me,
and I've learned that real love doesn't hurt.

I Tell You, "I Love You"

I tell you, "I love you."
And you say, "Mmmhmm."
I ask if you love me
and sarcastically you say,
"Oh, man, do I?"
I ask if you ever think you'll be
in love with me,
and you say, "Yeah."
I ask if you really care at all,
and you say,
"Can you talk about this tomorrow?"
I ask myself if I want to cry myself to sleep
one more night, wondering
why you don't love me and
why you can't be man enough to say it,
and I say, "No."

A Loss for Words

You usually show me a toughness,
but that's not who you are.
Lately, you've shown me a sweetness,
and I admit, I like it so far.

Recently, I've seen a side of you
that you have never shown,
and from this newfound closeness,
our friendship has really grown.

When life hits me hard,
you show me how to cope.
When I feel I can't go on,
you tell me there is hope.

When I see the darkness,
you see the light.
You won't let me give in,
not without a fight.

You're so far away,
yet so close to touch.
When you say kind words,
it helps me so much.

You say I have a gift,
for telling things untold,
that with my pen and paper,
my inner beauty unfolds.

Yes, I am a writer,
you know that much is true.
But words could not express
what I feel for you.

You truly are my best friend,
the one to whom I turn.
But more than your friendship
is for what I yearn.

I don't think it's impossible,
I don't think it's extreme.
I want to be your girl,
if only in my dreams.

You say you don't understand love
or what it's all about,
but if I were your girlfriend,
you would've already found out.

You say you're scared of love
and pain is not what you need,
but I guarantee you happiness
if you fall in love with me.

The Best

To have you once again,
to hold you now and then.

Thinking of it's such a stupid thing,
because to you I'm just a fling.

I loved you with all my heart and soul,
but you were the one to let go.

I've never loved anyone like this before,
and the strange thing is, now I love you more.

The look in your eyes, the touch of your face,
all of these things, my heart can't erase.

The love that I once had is now gone,
still, I don't have the strength to move on.

Again and again I ask myself, "Why?"
I was the best you ever had, wasn't I?

Another Sappy Love Poem

Why do I feel this way
when I know you don't feel for me?
I'm leading my heart in dismay,
but I'm just too blind to see.
They say that love is blind,
and I guess that that is true.
My heart is telling my mind
that I need to feel for you.
I wish I could open my eyes
and see what's really there.
My heart is telling me lies,
and I know that you don't care.
So I guess this was wasted time,
yet still you remain on my mind.

My Choice

Where do I begin? Or should I say where do I end?
I see in your eyes that I can only be a friend.

Does it hurt? Yes—to say no would be a lie,
and yes, without a doubt, every day I will cry.

You are the closest thing I have ever had to true love,
but I know when you look at me that's not what you're thinking of.

I can say now without a doubt, I know my Fate,
to live forever childless and without a mate.

Most people have one or the other to keep them strong,
I will have neither, but I will move on.

For you, I have sacrificed so much of who I am,
and I promised myself I would change for no man.

I have no dignity or respect left for myself.
I took who I am and put her on a shelf.

And for what? Some sex, and cuddling at night?
You're not in love with me, so it just isn't right.

Have I asked you to change for me at all?
No, I accepted you, shitty underwear and all.

I guess in some ways my dad was right about one thing.
I will never look at my hand and see a wedding ring.

No man could ever love me, how could they dare?
I'm too worthless and repulsive for anyone to care.

It's okay, though. I knew with you I was on borrowed time,
but at least for a little while I called you mine.

Even if it was just pretend, I liked playing your wife,
but as I said, Fate has a different course for my life.

One thing you are forgetting, baby, one thing you don't seem to understand—
you are not the only one who's giving the other a chance.

People rejected you time and time again.
You were loveless until I stepped in.

When others did not, I gave you the time of day,
but to you I'm only a friend, a sister, you say.

I can't do this, not anymore. It's my life and I do have a voice.
Who do I choose? Me, myself, and I—that is my choice.

I hope you find happiness in your endeavor for love,
and one day I won't be in your memory to think of.

But you will always be in mine,
for that one space in time.

When I had a chance to experience you cared,
but when I reach out, you won't be there.

It's okay. I've accepted the hand Fate has given to me,
and I wish you all the love you could never have for me.

So good luck and good-bye. I love you and will miss you, no doubt,
but I'm not waiting for your choice, because I've figured mine out.

Thanks for Nothing

You said you'd be there for me,
but you're not.
You said you were my friend,
but you forgot.

I'm tired of broken promises;
these excuses are getting old.
I want a real best friend,
not someone who leaves me cold.

I don't think you understand
just how much it hurts
to have your "best friend"
slam your face in the dirt.

Do me one more favor—
don't promise anymore dreams,
because everything you say
is a lie, it always seems.

A Chance

I love you so much, but I have to fake it.
I'm scared of rejection, I just can't take it.

I've been rejected by so many guys, so many times.
I wish I could tell if you like me, but I don't read minds.

I'm afraid you'll reject me because I'm not at all pretty or thin.
I know you say, "That's not true." But I hear it again and again.

That is why it's taken me ten months to say this:
my heart has been consumed by you in endless bliss.

When I think about your gorgeous blue eyes,
it makes me feel all warm and fuzzy inside.

When I think about the assholes I've dated in the past, I ask myself, "Why?"
Where have you been my whole life? You're such a sweet and wonderful guy.

I want to tell you that if you do not care for me, or have feelings for me too,
that I hope we can remain friends and talk on the phone, if that's all right with you.

What I'm really hoping and praying of
is that you'll say, "You are my one true love."

I would really like to have a shot at a true romance,
because I know I'm not perfect, but will you give me a chance?

Section Four:

Poems Of My Life, My Thoughts, And Me

The Life I've Never Known

It's funny how you think that things can never happen to you,
but it's not very funny when those things *do come true.*

You say to yourself, "That'll never happen to me, only to someone else,"
and as you say that, you put reality on the shelf.

You never know what the next day will bring,
so keep an open mind to everything.

Don't think it can't happen, because one day it will.
You'll know because your spine will get an awful chill.

I know because I speak from experience; it happened to me.
My dad quit his job and now we have no money.

It's hard to comprehend when you're used to spending money every day,
but now every penny has to be kept and saved.

I'm not saying we're poor, because, no, we aren't that.
I'm just saying there's no extra money; that's a fact.

It's tough when you hear your friends say where they went, or what
they got to do,
knowing that you're stuck at home and that's all just a dream to you.

When my dad quit his job he promised things wouldn't fall apart,
but he broke his promise, and with it, my heart.

He does small jobs here and there,
but that still doesn't get us anywhere.

When he broke his promise I lost all the respect for him I had.
I still love him, and always will because he's my dad.

I just wish he'd go look for a job and find something good.
I know that he could if he wanted to, and I wish he would.

Right now he might get disability, and we're getting stamps for food,
but we can't even go to the same stores, because people are mean and
crude.

I know that he feels bad and that is why he's depressed,
but to lay around and cry all day is nothing but wasted breath.

Sometimes he yells at me for no reason and just snaps;
afterwards he goes in his bedroom and takes a nap.

I don't know why he yells at me, or what it is I did.
I would go get a job if I could, but technically, I'm still a kid.

Sometimes when I'm around him, I can't help but feel ashamed
and wonder to myself if I'm the one to blame.

Maybe if I hadn't taken things for granted, I wouldn't feel so bad.
At least I can look back and see the good things that I had.

No, I'm not spoiled, I just want my old life back—is that too much to ask?
I want things the way they used to be, the way they were in the past.

If I would have though this could have happened to me, more gratefulness
I would have shown,
but I'm sorry to say I didn't think that way, so now I'm living the life I've
never known.

This Incredible Woman

This Incredible Woman my gratitude I owe.
This Incredible Woman has watched me as I grow.

This Incredible Woman in her life has been through hell.
This Incredible Woman has strength, and has taught me well.

This Incredible Woman picks me up after I fall.
This Incredible Woman has been there through it all.

This Incredible Woman makes me mad once in a while.
This Incredible Woman then somehow makes me smile.

This Incredible Woman has been there through all of my sorrows.
This Incredible Woman has shown me there's a better tomorrow.

This Incredible Woman has made me the woman I am today.
This Incredible Woman, a million thanks I would like to say.

This Incredible Woman has helped me in so many ways.
This Incredible Woman a billion dollars could not repay.

This Incredible Woman is intelligent, hardworking, and kind.
This Incredible Woman is by far the best friend I could find.

This Incredible Woman I would so much like to be.
This Incredible Woman has truly inspired me.

This Incredible Woman rises above all the rest.
This Incredible Woman has made me truly blessed.

This Incredible Woman is like no other.
This Incredible Woman is My Mother.

9-11-01

So much hatred, so much pain—
will the world be the same again?

How will we cope, how will we stand
when our lives are taken by Terror's hands?

The thought that justice will prevail
is a nice thought, but what if it fails?

Note to Jerry Falwell

After his comments on 9-11-01

Did you have a very traumatic childhood?
Because the things you say are misunderstood.

Doesn't our religion say not to judge?
It always seems like you hold a grudge

against those who have a different point of view,
but hardly anybody thinks like you.

You go to the extremes, and you may think you have class,
but really Jerry, you're talking out of your ass.

I mean, who cares about a Teletubby who carries a purse?
There are problems in this world a whole lot worse.

Recently, you attacked pagans, abortionists, and gays.
You on your high horse say, "They're the ones to blame!"

Where do you get that from, tell me? Where do you see
that they're in the wrong? They're OUR community!

In times like these, we need love and peace,
not some wacko evangelist trying to start heat.

Jerry, I know that what you say, you believe is true,
but the real terrorist threat to America is people like you!

Troubled World

Hate doesn't stop hate,
so why discriminate?

Help out each other;
don't let love suffer.

Hatred is a learned thing,
but don't let it bring

our country to its knees,
I'm begging you please.

If you don't let love live,
it might be your life you give.

The Color Black

People look at me and they stare; they think I'm weird.
They say, "Hey, look at her, she doesn't belong here."

People say I'm strange, and they think I'm possessed,
and it's all because of the way that I dress.

I wear the same color every single day.
It's what I like— I express myself this way.

It doesn't matter what people say or do,
what you want to wear is only up to you.

I don't let their opinions affect me.
If they would look past my clothes, then they'd see.

I'm not such a bad person after all,
even if I do dress off the wall.

Some people say that I worship the devil,
some people say that I look like a rebel.

Some people say that I dress like a mime,
but honestly, I think I look fine.

People are entitled to their own opinions.
It is a free country that we live in.

Everyone has their favorite color or shade,
but with mine, everyone thinks it's a phase.

I say it's not, it's what I like,
just like a person with a buzz or a spike.

It doesn't affect their personality,
it's just what they like and want to be.

Nobody picks on them or singles them out,
so why me? What's that all about?

The way I dress doesn't affect the way I act,
just because I like to wear the color black.

Loneliness Is a Disease

LONELINESS   is a   DISEASE.
Some can recover,
Some can't.
I can <u>not</u>.
It scares me.
The anxiety of no one being there.
I hate that.
Heart pounding,
Butterflies.
Will it get better?
Or more difficult?
Only in   TIME,
I'll find,
The   CURE.

Today Is My Birthday

Today is my birthday,
but I'm just one in five billion.

Today is my birthday,
and I got three phone calls.

Today is my birthday,
and I got two presents.

Today is my birthday.
I got nothing from Grandma.

Today is my birthday,
and I got hung up on by my best friend.

Today is my birthday,
and I got three cards.

Today is my birthday,
and two of my friends didn't want to talk.

Today is my birthday,
and I only got one hug, from my mom.

Today is my birthday.
I had ice cream and cake, but no party.

Today is my birthday.
I didn't make a wish.

Today is my birthday,
and it was the shittiest day of my life.

Today is my birthday,
but nobody cares, because I'm nobody, right?

A Small Prayer

I say my prayers every night,
like a good Christian should.
I pray that God will show me the light,
and help me out if He would.

I guess I'm going through hard times,
that's why I'm so depressed.
I pray that everything will be fine,
if God knows that that's best.

I don't have any friends,
and I'm not telling a lie
I thought that friends were till the end.
The reason they left, I don't know why.

My grades are dropping in school.
I guess my nerves are wacked.
I know that I'm not a fool,
and I hope I'll get back on track.

I'm also having family trouble,
mostly with my father,
but starting a fight only makes it double,
so we don't talk—why bother?

I'd like to lose weight and be thin.
I try to lose it, yet I always fail.
It seems like a battle I can't win,
so I guess I'll always look like a whale.

I'd like to have a new boyfriend,
but people say I'm too shy.
I guess I'm still in love with my old one,
and when I think about him I cry.

I'd like to get started on my music career,
but it seems like I'm getting nowhere.
I know I could make it in a year,
but people say, "No", that's just not fair.

But most of all I'd like self-confidence
so maybe I won't be so scared,
because everyone knows in the least sense,
without it, you will get nowhere.

I'm only fifteen, I don't need this,
not for a few more years anyway.
I pray that *God* will take it from me,
and maybe I'll handle it someday.

My Virginity

I'm going to tell you a story, and I am telling you the truth.
My ex-boyfriend pressured me to do something I didn't want to do.

I got scared and stayed quiet after we broke up,
but now I think it's time for me to speak out and open up.

If I say "No," I can call it attempted rape,
and I will if I have to, for my virginity's sake.

I don't care if a guy says, "Come on, let's do it."
I want to wait until marriage, and I'm gonna prove it.

If a girl says "No," a guy gets mad with hatred,
but it doesn't bother me, not with something this sacred.

I don't care what guys say or think,
it's not going to be my reputation that sinks.

People say losing your virginity is cool and fun,
but they all wish they had it back, when it's over and done.

If you are a virgin you get more respect,
and in this world you need all that you can get.

Trust me, if a guy really truly cares,
if you say "No," he'll stay right there.

Guys are out to get one thing and one thing alone—
they're not going to be there when the baby comes home.

I haven't ever done anything but kiss,
and believe me, sex is last on my list.

I could catch HIV and die of AIDS—
then who will I turn to if I'm alone or afraid?

I could get pregnant, and have a baby.
I'm only fifteen—people will think I'm crazy.

Protection isn't always the key.
Am I getting my point across? Now do you see?

I've been there, girls, listen to me.
This is why I don't want to lose my virginity.

The Last Afternoon of My Life

On the last afternoon of my life,
I hope to be with my family,
to tell them all that I love them and hold them,
to say one last good-bye to my close friends.

On the last afternoon of my life,
I hope to make peace with God above,
to right all my wrongs,
to reminisce on the good things in my life.

On the last afternoon of my life,
I hope to know that I made a difference somehow,
to have touched just one person, in one way,
to believe that the world will go on.

On the last afternoon of my life,
I hope to live.

Maybe It's Better

The pain
of being denied
what I thought was love
was not true.
Not even a friend
to lean on.
They've all gone.
I guess I'm too deep for them.
No one will ever understand
what's in my soul
but me.

Nobody's Perfect

I wonder if I'll ever be normal.
If you define normal, I guess nobody is.

I wonder if I'll ever lose my weight.
But different sizes are what shape the world.

I wonder if I'll ever be beautiful.
Then again, not everyone is born to be a super model.

I wonder if I'll ever be famous.
Yet, some people are—in their own minds.

I wonder if I'll ever have a "lasting" relationship.
Maybe I really do have a soul mate.

I wonder if I'll ever get married.
Hey, half of all marriages end in divorce.

I wonder if I'll ever have children.
But then I'd have to grow up too.

I wonder if I'll ever become president.
People have said I should be in politics.

I wonder if I'll ever be truly free.
Because everything has a cost.

I wonder if I'll ever be respected.
You have to give respect to get respect.

I wonder if I'll ever be accepted for who I am.
Because, hey, nobody's perfect.